I0756332

FINISHING LINE PRESS
www.finishinglinepress.com

Through the Wreckage

selected poems by

J.T. Trigonis

Finishing Line Press
Georgetown, Kentucky

Through the Wreckage

Because I've owed this to myself. (And more so to others.)

ISBN 979-8-89990-380-9 First Edition

ACKNOWLEDGMENTS

Versions of "Old '89" have been published in print in *Harpur Palate, Afterword*, and most recently in *The Red Wheelbarrow*, as well as online at *The Good Men Project*. In 2024, the poem was also included as part of the TEXT-FOR-POEM initiative. "Old '89" was a Top Ten finalist in the Poetry Super Highway Poetry Contest

"Revisiting Corso" has been published in print in the anthology *Arcade of the Scribes*

"Ouroboros" has been published in print in *The Red Wheelbarrow*

"The Naked Kiss" has been published online by The Good Men Project

"Emerge" has been published in print in the anthology *Arcade of the Scribes*

"Time Capsules" has been published in print in *Teaneck Poetry Park*

A version of "Roadhouse" has been published in print in *The Chaffin Journal* and *Pennsylvania English*

"Princes II Kings" has been published online by *Quagmire Magazine*

"Brokendown Love" has been published in print in *Black Book Press*

"At Closing Time" has been published in print in *Iodine Poetry Journal* and online at The Good Men Project

Publisher: Leah Huete de Maines
Editor: Christen Kincaid
Cover Art: *Alien* by Kaitlin Buccini
Author Photo: Marinell C. Montales
Cover Design: Marinell C. Montales

Order online: www.finishinglinepress.com

Author inquiries and mail orders:
Finishing Line Press
PO Box 1626
Georgetown, Kentucky 40324
USA

Contents

I have measured out my life with coffee spoons
—T.S. Eliot, The Love Song of J. Alfred Prufrock

***

There is a crack, a crack in everything
That's how the light gets in
—Leonard Cohen, Anthem

***

Mercy mercy, Mr. Percy, there ain't nothing back in Jersey
But a broken-down jalopy of a man I left behind
—Tom Waits, Invitation to the Blues

OLD '89

Crashed my lightning blue '89 Cavalier into the 1&9
divide after the Giants won Superbowl XLII.

So I wandered the Jersey City underworld, cloud heavy
passed motorcycle hangovers and White Mana

thinking how a lonesome star like mine could get the
moon's attention without police and hospital

lights on my tail to sweep up the busted glass—and
me—off someone else's powdered lines.

Everybody's drunk tonight, Saturn-ringed, speeding
with some sweet heartache wrapped around a

tattooed arm like a worn out Timex or a cheap bomb.
I think about the snapshots of my autopsy haunting

the front page of the *Journal*, my little roadside diversion
loitering the Youtube expanse for Stoned-Age

frat boys with nothing better to do than record my last
minutes for their 15 of fame, my own cheated for a

late night thumbsucker, platinum second mate in heels,
says she's been searching for a strong sailor with an

ashtray heart so she can burn away the last of her regrets.
What else can you say to an offer like that when

you're dizzied off a 12-pack of Bud, lost in the beautiful
car crash beneath the bridges of her eyebrows?

Sure, I tell her. *I'll put out the pain, Love. In both of us.*

REVISITING CORSO

after Gregory Corso's I am 25

The lines you left behind,
gasoline-choked like runaway girls on a
drunken heap of downfallen roses
ready for the match.

Those sad stories you graffitied onto my
brain, dug holes eternities deep into
my essence as a poet. Yet…

I fear I've become a reflection of
those old poetmen you so violently despised
when you were 25…

You can't knock me out and
I can't shake you,
like a ghost at 12 Ash St. Place.

But I sleep with the lights on; like John Lurie,
I shut my eyes, keep weapons
at my side every night

and especially on your birthday.

OUROBOROS

I dropped 30¢ and a letter on a sandwich he left at the bar,
took a bite because it needed taking under the
hot sun lamps—smut on my nose. That 30¢
should be enough to buy a one way phone call to
another time. Same bar. New me?

And the letter?

That's good for a lap dance, some laughs or her love
on the side streets of a smart phone world, where
dreams walk with medusa-eyed muses and poets
Lethe away past sips, sleep off tomorrow's sins
against a bar wet with serpents

eating their own tails…

The bite in my sandwich. 30¢ and a letter. Unread. *Again.*

THE NAKED KISS

It was a naked kiss shared between two nobodies
in the night, moonlight vinyl scratching

into a cracked ceiling where crystal chandeliers
once lit up letters and lovers alike.

The front door ached with every turn of
their heads, as two strangers' tongues tried to

pick the locks into the dark mysteries of each other,
TV salt and peppered, the ice rumbling

rhythmic in broken glasses on the night table.
A naked kiss and nothing more, she said.

In the fanless dark, shadows chased themselves as
stray *I love you*s danced broken record on

airwaves around their twisted bodies on the zombie
bed they tried desperately not to crease.

She eavesdropped for an ex's engine revving in the lot
while used car salesman's eyes scanned

thick curtains for the owl-shaped headlights of a '57
Ford Thunderbird. *A naked kiss*, she said...

But the way they loved away that rug-burnt evening in
Room 314 of the Horizon Motel was both warm as

childhood and Willy Loman cold, meant being caught
in a gorgon's gaze and never blinking.

He, content with puckered lips; she with kissing stone.

PURPLE

I was once asked,
what color is that poem?
and the color that manifested
was not the memory-crusted
hue of the car
in the poem
(lightning blue) but

purple.
The color of telepathy.
of my spirit animal.
of my spurned loves and losses.
Color of loyalty,
of frivolity,
whose scent is
scratch-n'-sniff Ben & Jerry's
mixed with
public enemy number one.
A taste for setting suns;
of setting forth from
San Francisco to San Diego
sans sweethearts
or cherry Chapstick
or hydrogen bomb-suits.
Only thick layers of

purple.
A color unearthed through
deep space meditation,
wrapped in blue velvet
radio static symposiums and
covered up by black hole clusters,
yet uncovered by Ken Nordine's
spoken word.
A tinge of impossible longings,
belongings,
infertility,

Infidelities;
the colorlessness of a
world without stars
while We Await Silent Trystero's
Empire, a purple W.A.S.T.E.land
that becomes the journey of
the bullet that killed
Brandon Lee.
A shade of ghost whose sound is
shackles
around the wrists of this
unconscious guilt for being
there—and here—even *now*—with
nothing broken enough
to fix.

Or, if broken at all,
not needing a new set of
Goodyears in purple's
presence—color of sex, death,
and M. Night Shyamalan;
a mechanized muse's moonbeam
eyes made icy by midnight quiets which
no light can color.
No purple conversations
or lightning blue
Cavaliers
or black, thundering
Celebrities or any of the other
silver-lined Chevies left to the
dust of a not-so-long ago lost youth
and most certainly not
the unbroken, damn near
unbreakable ink spots
of this poem.

But...
do *I* make purple, or
does the poem blend purple
out of red and blue?
Out of *me*. And out of you, too.

AN INESCAPABLE SMILE

Prison bars built between
Neruda-soft lips.
Polyester eyebrows rise,
elastic on high.

She muses what thoughts
a snowflake thinks as
it melts beneath the heat
of salt or Dickinson's tears.

A café troubadour strums
a chord in the key of she,
and it lingers in the air,
a gaze through the crack in
the glass of he.
Eyes all Pessoa brown and
just as melancholy,

immaculate.

WE ARE NOT BULLETPROOF

Her body, ensconced in bubble wrap.
A watchful pendulum sways.
The rusted rocking horse or porch swing
on which kisses are passed
between whispers and time.

Somewhere, a trap is set.
Somewhere else, a bullet smiles at
1700 MPH, and
we are not immune to
gunmetal or lipstick.

With red stains on our collars,
we drift off to jobs,
mummified in cotton and polyester
to be crucified by work.

A quiet pendulum.
Runaway horses in a barn enraptured
by flame or fantasy.
We enter this night as ourselves,
exit as someone else,

and no less bulletproof than before.

CALLAHAN'S NIGHTS

Denise would slip me a Bud heavy after a 16-hour
shift slinging burgers and fries at the

Meadowlands Flea when I was six years shy of
drinking age. Two years later, I sat squirming six

inches from her course Catholic curvature on her
mother's loveseat watching *East Enders* until 3

in the morning. It was 19 degrees with a chance of
Bermuda Triangle. I couldn't make out the signposts

planted like aluminum sunflowers in the blue-gray
Hackensack of her suburbanite eyes, so I inched

closer in the blackness of each commercial break.
Her world was paved with road kill and rot,

pebbled with ivory feathers and the nightmare-gnawed
bones of innocence. I retraced my fingertrails

through her hair after a brief collision of lips beneath
the fwoosh of Rte. 46, her father blacked-out beside

a worn-out *Rainbow Bright* pillowcase and all five
New Kids on the Block her walls would eventually tire

of holding up with time. The vacancy of the Callahan's
lot became a padre to whom I repented countless

missed calls from her mouth to mine, the fluorescent
all-beef lamplight awaiting a deep-fried atonement

for all the jokes we didn't get in that British sitcom,
now lying fallen, cold, and unfunny at my feet.

Next morning the road home lay pockmarked with
blood-drained sermons, crushed metal once

tuned to the shape of her favorite flower reflecting that
night, still, and ever parted before me—

an unswimmable sea tattooed with her unsinkable
moonlight.

HAM-AND-EGGERS AT THE HEARTBREAK CAFE

We were broken glasses at the Heartbreak Café
shoveling ham and eggs and a side of

sleepless nights into our tired mouths, our burnt neon
eyes staring blindly beyond the Melba toast.

She's not a high-heel kinda girl, Sham marbled
through crunching toast and a Main Line smile that

wouldn't derail. *Boots and full body tattoos. That's
her style.* I thumbed through an e.e. cummings

collection he'd attested got him laid and left him
limp as a pair of socks on a clothesline.

Sham coughed—*I was a rusty old Dodge, man!*
I stared at his tea bag washed up like a dead

anchor beside its cup and thought about the poor
malnourished fern I've nursed for 20 years.

I uncapped a flask that shields my chest from
stray bullets and bloody nail polish.

Let's get these drinks up on their feet, I say and drip
a drab in each by the red light of the café sign,

the "T" flashing Morse code into the dead heavens
shipwrecking the next Savior who'd happen by.

Here's to love, my friend laughed, sipped and spilt the
Irish gold down his stubbly chin.

The waitress ambled over as waitresses often do, zeroed
in on my empty cup with the coffee pot in her

rattlesnake hand as an old Billy Joel b-side queued up.
No thanks, I said. *I'm fine. For now.*

EMERGE

You can't emerge
when you're unwilling to submerge
yourself into unknown depths
of self. Starless.
Existing as two halves
split down a center that
cannot hold consciousness
whole.

You'll never emerge
without diving down low
into the hell that hinders you,
allow yourself to orange like
that old Chevy, four flats and
a crack in the windshield
as wide as the universe is weary,
stranded in someone else's driveway.

Someone you don't recognize.

Someone whose company
you don't enjoy anymore.

Whose touch reminds you of
mind control.

Whose eyes, when kissed by
moonlight, are the color of longing.

Whose lips have misplaced
your name. *Again.*

And *that* is why all you can do
is dream of emergence
until something else
arises from within,
hotwires that fireless engine,

rides off onto the parkway
on wheels that time and breath
had all but forgot.

Rust and Ragnarok be damned.

TIME CAPSULES

It's the way warm crystals drop from
your mouth mistaking themselves
as gentle storms along my back,
the sleepless nights we sift through in
secret that we might dig up the
memory boxes we buried together
as children (*then*) with
thousands of miles between us
somehow seeming a thousand and one
times closer.

It's the way you shift your eyes
in my direction, how only you can
ever know these dimples as intimately
as falling stars know the ground
on which they humbly land, unseen
except by those pure of spirit.

It's how that once in a lifetime
happens once during every lifetime
though it's only in *this one* we remember
its happening.

How fortunate am I then,
to recollect it all,
dimples blossoming by the light of
your shooting stars, splitting skies
like moons eclipsed, eyes opened
to receive the storms,

In the sleeplessness between us,
we bury time capsules to one day
unearth a thousand times
and a thousand and one miles
from here, more than children (*now*)
yet nothing less brilliant
than dust tailing fallen stars across
a universe ever so needful of its light.

ROADHOUSE

We met at a roadhouse just outside Detroit,
where the Cadillac Circus pitched its

tents while geeks and dwarves drank moonshine
until they sang the same main line rag.

She told me her name was Ida, and I believed
her, lugged her busted old Million Miler

fattened up with brokendown lingerie and a
stack of battered *LA Times*

headlining her a "West Coast Sensation!" some
million miles behind: November 15, 1983.

The joint was empty except for a few ghosts
in the floorboards and my lovely pianist

playing that same song, her voice a crumpled
baritone despite a C-cup physique.

What's that one called? I ask, and she drags slow
motion on the Black & Mild caught

between her lips, smoke fogging up the tollbooths
of her eyes into a lonesome interstate heart.

One For My Baby, she replies, caught in a moment,
absent as the ring on the finger that matters.

But you wouldn't know now, would you?
No. No, I wouldn't.

And the piano played on without her.

HEAVY CREAM

The reflection in the napkin dispenser told me it was
over. I knew by the way

the salt and pepper shakers lost their black and white
between slender fingers that moments ago

dialed through the little black book in her heart.
Coffee, I wisp to the waitress, her pen poised

for further friction, ballpoint to pad, like the friction
between two bodies pumping, drained of fuel

beneath AC and HBO, in slow yet so out-of-touch.
She scratched its arid tip on the page, then

tucked it into her apron, withdrew a Bic Comfort Grip
from one of those graveyard pockets of hers.

That's all. Just coffee. The old glass bottle of Heinz
tried to preach its tomato paste truths.

I listen like the placemats listen, already imprinted
with stories not so easily discarded.

Milk or half-and-half? The waitress continues as my
companion files bits of broken bacon strips

into her mouth. One left, crumbling in her greasy embrace.
Milk is too light, I mused inside, and comes in

too many varieties—2%, 1%, low fat, skim—nothing's whole
anymore. And what's the point of half-and-half

when your heart's as heavy as maple syrup, leaden like the
Cupid-tipped anchor that keeps us docked and dining,

keeps me passing through the revolving door to sit and sip away the
midnight ghosts of yet another after-love affair morning?

PRINCES II KINGS

There's so much debris, shards of our former
selves lay dormant. Now, only radio edits

remain. We watched our Frank Sinatras die
along the Hudson-Bergen Light Rail, so

I tune to those frequencies that refuse change
its rite of passage. The unknowingness of

what's to come fills me with false heirs and bold
typeface prophecies, the Parkway buck

left to rot while I coddled a Cleopatra-shaped
dent in my hood, a bruised, bashful ego, and

a lay I'd never bask in any knuckle-gnarled
glow after our four hours were up.

We gasolined brittle leftovers of an epic poem,
kept warm atop Levi-faded rooftops and

7-11s serving Slurpees until the ground below
chipped away at the guitar-string guillotine

mapping our palms in shadow puppet memoir.
We were a pair of street corner conquerors

questing for Coca-Cola and something more shiny
to sacrifice the night to than ourselves.

Still we wait, as written—once princes, now kings
glued like gold to cracked star-kingdoms

watching tomorrow's scions inherit these sacred
thrones which we never left, just got up from

momentarily to stretch our legs. See what else
might be burning white nebula and bright

far, far beyond our own calamitous little world.

VAULT, ALLURED

Fire-eaters and world-swallowers
stalk these shell-shocked
slivers of street, Jersey City, with
bitches a-brew beneath a
berserker's bassline
bouldering lamentations from the
Ninth Circle of Miles Davis.

Beneath shards of reflection in a six-eyed
moon, serpent-dagger fangs Excalibur
into Eden's long dead stump,
poisoning our Paradise cores with an
impeccable malady

called *Life.*

These heights toward which we aspiral,
funereal pyres packed with
quiet corpses under bridges,
far above the big top
and lazy sun,
flutter down diamonds and promises,
each, upon landing, more delicate
than the last.

And we, with moondust in our eyes,
wander in a bat-blind
depthlessness Jerusalemed in this
double agent Christ of night,

shimmer past the much too infrequent
3 AM lamplight music-mosaic
as if we were nothing less
magnanimous

than crucified stars.

BROKENDOWN LOVE

Brokendown affections defogged on a dislocated shoulder,
dusty Turnpike tires pancaked by deerskin flashbacks,

shattered rearview, wheels gone AWOL with unreadable
warranties. Chipped paint and crushed garlic croutons

loiter on the backseat floor, remnants of a relationship gone
far, now further back than the last roadside siren.

Sunvisors worn dead by heat stroke, mascara claw marks,
Chuck Taylors awash in beach weekends or sports bras,

glove box to trunk rifled through. Between bumper stickers
and B.B. King I found her burgundy chalice (hair like

Seattle rain, blood wine or transmission oil), pristine yet dark,
secretly knotted by a moist and muddled Gordian fault.

Here, busted taillight lovers dance on sun-draped dashboards
nearest my exit wound. The rest stop dreamer in any city,

off every freeway, tans away his asphalt heartache to ash and
oil-dyed dungarees, the dithered choices of a motel sign,

every light burnt black but the letter "T" awaiting a crucifixion—
something—while the everyday emptiness refuels.

AT CLOSING TIME

I watch the little red-headed Filipina
collect the candles from the cafe tabletops
and blow them out one by one.

All except *mine.* Without a glance, she assumes
I need the light.

That's how you know you've become
a *regular*—when the waitress keeps a flame
burning for you at 9:54 PM,
your coffee cold, but still as dark,
the sugar packets porcelain abodes refilled,
forks and knives wrapped tightly in
tomorrow morning's napkins.

That's how you know. When it's time to go but
no one sends you home.

When they let you blow out your own candle.

OLD '95

Raged that old silver '95 on midnight oil slicks,
Jersey City to Asbury—

she, my Sylvia Plath, and me in driver's bucket
seat working Cavalier spurs into floor mat,

dodging antimatter potholes, ducking whirlwinds
all down dark Garden State parkways,

E-Z Pass emerald pathways. All the while, shy
glances paralyzed me from inside the

chastised bottles we spun as youth-filled fools,
her eyes lit up gold beyond the long-grown

shadows of Exit 102. My free hand slipped into
the in-between where thighs burn smoothest,

damp with the sour-sweet vintage of ancestral
regret. She laughed away my fireflies,

dealt a dozen tall Tarot card tales of futures retold,
and I couldn't help wondering:

out of how many rooms have these stubborn
Docs stormed, away from her?

Our unsteady hands felt our way across backseat
conversations; we lost our names to the black

hole glove box drifting off with omnipresent phone
chargers, asteroids, and a broken haiku.

She, ghost-poet narcotic, permanent poltergeist of
these eternal engine-light confessionals; my

St. America anchored to a sunken chest wrapped
in long goodbyes written in reverse,

no vacancy for leftover shards of second-hand China
that would welcome us home to old replayable

wars no more.

CHECK, PLS.

Evening checks lined up
(sponsored by American Express).
Yawns arrive like
consecutive tides
taking their time to crash.
Struggling in low-light buzz,
a vintage poet drones on
of times and of places
only he can revisit, can
return home to
upon paying the check.

In three parts.

Again.

SPECIAL THANKS

—Marinell, my love, for keeping me going
—Cheddar and Colby-Jack (because: cats)
—Raul, for holding me accountable
—James F. Broderick, my greatest champion
—John Dailey and Dr. Chris Wessman, mentors always
—Finishing Line Press, for putting this body of verse out there
—Film noir, Tom Waits, and all the pork pies I've ever worn
—All the used cars I've ever owned
—All the (minor) scars I've ever known

J.T. Trigonis (he/him) is a neon troubadour of the written and spoken word. With the obligatory MFA in poetry writing from Brooklyn College, an even more obligatory Pushcart Prize nomination, and a single written-on rejection slip from *The New Yorker* beckoning he send more, his poems have seen print in over five dozen magazines and journals that have made appearances on the bottom shelf of bookstands since 1998. Many of these poems are included in this very collection. Some of his favorites include *Harpur Palate, California Quarterly, Rockland Review, Barbaric Yawp, Poetry Salzburg, Iodine Poetry, Evansville Review, Red Wheelbarrow,* and *By the WAYE.* He has also had poetry published online, too, namely at *Empty Mirror* and *The Good Men Project.* Trigonis is the author of six self-published chapbooks, which include his *Warehouse City* trilogy (*Blues, Noir,* and *Western*), *5th Avenue Bomb in the Covergirl Heart,* and *androids with angel faces.* His micro chapbook *What Great Stars and Other Poems* was published by In Hindsight Press in 2021.

Since the mid-nineties, Trigonis has been an integral part of the open mic poetry scene in New Jersey and NYC and has headlined at over four dozen venues. These include Art House Productions, The Waterbug Hotel, Monochrome Mondays, Backroom Broadsides, the Silver-Tongued Devils and Phoenix Reading series, NYC Poetry Fest, Hudson County and Jersey City Poetry Festivals, and the Wordbeat, Grantwood, Red Wheelbarrow, and River Read series. Trigonis also plays master of ceremonies at WAYE (short for "We Appreciate Your Enthusiasm"), a monthly poetry reading series he and his partner host at their vintage shop/used bookstore Sure Things in Jersey City Heights. They are also the publishers of *By the WAYE*, a magazine of poetry and visual art..

Aside from poetry, Trigonis has had some of his flash and micro fiction published online at The Horror Tree and Black Hare Press's "Dark Moments," and in print in *Nunum's Done in a Hundred* anthology. He is a freelance writing and public speaking professor, as well as the author of the acclaimed book *Crowdfunding for*

Filmmakers, published in 2013 and 2016 (second edition) by Michael Wiese Productions and is a world-renowned authority on the titular subject.

He lives in Jersey City Heights with his partner and their two orange tabbies.

FOLLOW ME: @trigonis and @waye_poetry on Instagram
WEBSITE: thejohntrigonis.com

www.ingramcontent.com/pod-product-compliance
Lightning Source LLC
LaVergne TN
LVHW090541110826
845146LV00003B/1211

* 9 7 9 8 8 9 9 9 0 3 8 0 9 *